Let's Look at Lizards

BEARDED DRAGONS

By Seth Lynch

Gareth Stevens
PUBLISHING

Please visit our website, www.garethstevens.com. For a free color catalog of all our high-quality books, call toll free 1-800-542-2595 or fax 1-877-542-2596.

Library of Congress Cataloging-in-Publication Data
Names: Lynch, Seth, author.
Title: Bearded dragons / Seth Lynch.
Description: Buffalo, New York : Gareth Stevens Publishing, [2025] |
    Series: Let's look at lizards! | Includes index.
Identifiers: LCCN 2023034779 | ISBN 9781538292679 (library binding) | ISBN
    9781538292662 (paperback) | ISBN 9781538292686 (ebook)
Subjects: LCSH: Bearded dragons (Reptiles)–Juvenile literature.
Classification: LCC QL666.L223 L96 2025 | DDC 597.95/5–dc23/eng/20230828
LC record available at https://lccn.loc.gov/2023034779

First Edition

Published in 2025 by
Gareth Stevens Publishing
2544 Clinton Street
Buffalo, NY 14224

Editor: Kristen Nelson
Designer: Leslie Taylor

Photo credits: Cover, p. 15 Ken Griffiths/Shutterstock.com; p. 5 Anari/Shutterstock.com; p. 7 Camilo Torres/ Shutterstock.com; p. 9 Cre8tive Images/Shutterstock.com; p. 11 (green) Katoosha/Shutterstock.com, (red) Apisak P/Shutterstock.com, (yellow) Jennifer Yount Photo/Shutterstock.com; p. 13 Agus_Gatam/Shutterstock. com; p. 17 Vic Rincon/Shutterstock.com; p. 19 New Africa/Shutterstock.com; p. 21 Dudley Simpson/ Shutterstock.com; p. 23 Virginia Blount/Shutterstock.com.

Printed in the United States of America

CPSIA compliance information: Batch #CS25GS: For further information contact Gareth Stevens, New York, New York at 1-800-542-2595.

Find us on

Contents

Let's Look at
      Bearded Dragons 4

Lizard Life......................6

A Fun Tail 16

Baby Beardies...............20

Words to Know 24

Index.........................24

Which lizard is this?
It's a bearded dragon!

They have scales.
They have a "beard"!

Their neck
changes color.
It can turn light or dark.
This means they are
warm or cold.

They can be tan
or yellow.
They can be green
or red.

They have long tails.

They live in deserts.
They hide
in the ground.

They eat bugs and fruit.

They can be kept
as pets.
They like to be held!

Mothers lay eggs.
They are as big as
a grape.

Babies grow fast.
They shed their skin
as they grow.